SEARCH
FOR STEAM

British Rail 1951–1962

CHARLIE VERRALL

AMBERLEY

First published 2019

Amberley Publishing
The Hill, Stroud
Gloucestershire, GL5 4EP

www.amberley-books.com

British Library Cataloguing in Publication Data.
A catalogue record for this book is available from the British Library.

ISBN 978 1 4456 8519 9 (print)
ISBN 978 1 4456 8520 5 (ebook)

Typeset in 10pt on 12pt Sabon.
Origination by Amberley Publishing.
Printed in the UK.

Contents

Introduction

By the late 1950s the motive power in use by British Railways, both on passenger and freight services, was changing fast. Much of the marshalling yard shunting was performed by diesel shunters, diesel and electric multiple units were very much in evidence on many local services, and further electrification had taken place or was in the planning stages.

From 1958 onward, new, larger diesel locomotives were being introduced, which started to replace steam locomotives of a similar size. This was ironic since the manufacture of the various standard steam designs introduced from 1951 had only just been completed; in fact, construction of the Class 9 freight locomotives would continue until 1960. The result of these changes was to be the elimination of standard gauge steam on British Railways in 1968.

A third-generation railwayman based at Croydon on the Southern Region, I decided in mid-1961 to augment my earlier railway photographs by obtaining a series of trackside permits, together with permission to visit some locomotive sheds, and start recording steam workings on some of the main lines radiating out of London. Even at that stage, withdrawals and movements away from the London area of familiar locomotive types had commenced.

As a schoolboy I lived adjacent to the London to Brighton main line, by Wivelsfield station. In addition, from 1948 until 1953 I went by train each day to school in Hove, passing the locomotive works at Brighton and, of course, Brighton sheds. Brighton works were finishing off building the last of the West Country 4-6-2s, to be followed by a batch of Fairburn Class 4 2-6-4 tanks and the majority of the BR Standard Class 4 tanks, and the infamous Leader Class locos. In 1951 Brighton shed was still home to many ex-LBSCR locomotives, plus a fleet of West Country Class engines mainly used for the services to Plymouth and Cardiff, the heaviest freights to London and the newspapers trains. Heady days indeed.

Following the electrification of the London to Brighton main line in the 1930s, there were few scheduled steam-hauled passenger services to be seen, mainly just the Newhaven Boat Trains hauled by King Arthur Class 4-6-0s or Marsh Atlantics, and later on by one of the Southern Railway Co-Co electric locos, together with the Inter-Regional services to the South Coast from Birkenhead and Wolverhampton. The latter were usually the responsibility of ex- SECR D Class 4-4-0s. Freight services were all steam-hauled, although being at school during the day I was to see very few of them, except one that preceded my train to school. In the early days this was invariably hauled by WD 2-8-0 No. 77007; later on it was usually either a C2x 0-6-0 or a K Class 2-6-0.

Brighton shed was often visited on a Saturday, or rather viewed from Platforms 1 and 2, where a gaggle of schoolboys were always present. Quite frequently arrangements were made to drag lines of stored locos out of the depths of the shed for us to see. At this time all I had was a box camera, but from 1951 on I tried to record some of what I saw up until I started work as a trainee booking clerk at Hassocks station, after which my spotting and photographic opportunities became limited, with no more trips to the London termini. Sadly all the logs of where and when different locomotives were seen over the years have been lost.

From 1949 until 1953 I belonged to a locospotters club that ran Sunday coach tours round many of the London engine sheds, although I cannot remember visiting any of those of the Southern Region. These trips were a spotters paradise: Stratford, with almost all the allocation present plus the works crane tanks and engines waiting to enter or just ex-works; King's Cross Top Shed full of Pacifics and quite often the unique W1 4-6-4; Old Oak Common, again much of the full allocation; Neasden with many Great Central types; and of course Willesden, Cricklewood and Kentish Town, where in fact there were too many locos close together to get decent photographs. It really is a shame my lists of that period have not survived, since they would have made for interesting reading.

In addition I also went on many visits with friends, one of whom gave me some pages of his photographs when he stopped spotting. One visit was in either April or May 1949

LNER Y4 Class No. 68127 at Stratford in 1950. (C. F. Verrall collection, photographer not known)

SER B1 Class No. 1448 at Ashford in May 1949. (C. F. Verrall collection, photographer not known)

Diesel shunter No. 15227 and Fell diesel No. 10100 at Eastbourne in June 1951. (C. F. Verrall collection, photographer not known)

LBSCR B4x Class No. 2055 at Eastbourne sheds in June 1951. (C. F. Verrall collection, photographer not known)

to Ashford, where we saw several South Eastern Railway engines, including B1 No. 1448, O1 No. 1429 and R1 No. 31107. Also seen were two Southern diesel shunters, Nos 15214 and 15215, which were awaiting completion. Another visit we made, which I did not photograph, was to Eastbourne in June 1951 when the International Timetable Convention was being held. A number of new British Railways locomotives were on view from the station platforms, including Britannia Class No. 70009 *Alfred the Great*, Class 5 No. 73001 (both hauled into position by E4 Class 2485 in Southern livery), diesel shunter No. 15227 coupled to Fell 4-8-4 diesel No. 10100, and Standard 4 4-6-0 No. 75000. Also stored in Eastbourne sheds were a number of B4x 4-4-0s, including Nos 32042, 2055 and 2060.

Chapter One

Early Photographs: 1951–1955

All the early photographs were taken using a box camera – not the ideal vehicle for railway photography, especially moving trains. With its fixed slow speed, no focusing and no aperture control, it is surprising that any images worth retaining were obtained. Nowadays, of course, everyone is a photographer, with a wide range of digital cameras available from simple point and shoot to complex, expensive lens and body combinations. In fact, good quality images can be obtained from the camera on many smartphones.

Many of my early photographs were taken in the Brighton area and on family holidays in South Devon. One of the early Devon visits was to Plymouth North Road on 7 May 1951, where among other locomotives seen were No. 7029 *Clun Castle*, working the 13.00 to Liverpool Lime Street, 4575 Class No. 5567 and 6400 Class No. 6414. Staying in South Devon, my next visit was in September 1952, firstly on the 7th to Newton Abbot, where King Class No. 6017 *King Edward IV* was seen on the Down relief road waiting for a pilot, probably a Grange Class, for the climbs between Newton Abbot and Plymouth. Seen later in the Down relief road was 5101 Class No. 5108 on an engineers' train, while in the Up bay 1400 Class No. 1435 was waiting to work a service to Moretonhampstead. Later, on the 11th, Hall Class No. 6934 *Beachamwell Hall* was photographed skirting the river approach to Teignmouth with an Up local service. My last visit to South Devon with a box camera was in July 1953; having started full-time employment, going on family holidays proved difficult. On the 2nd I visited Exeter Central, where No. 34029 *Lundy* was seen entering with an Up train breasting the steep climb from St David's; at St David's, Castle Class No. 7029 *Clun Castle* worked the 13.45 Bristol to Penzance; finally, at Newton Abbot 9400 Class No. 8403 was seen, as well as Castle Class No. 5057 *Earl Waldegrave*, which was working the 7.30 Paddington to Penzance.

Returning to my home area, there were several photographs taken at Brighton, including E6 Class No. 32413, E5 Class No. 32585, the last I1x, No. 2002, and Brighton-built LMS Class 4 tank No. 42094 all on 21 July 1951. On 27 July 1951, H Class No. 31310 and D3 Class No. 32365 were seen; the last I3 Class No. 32091 was spotted on 25 February 1952; and H2 Class Atlantic No. 32422 *North Foreland* was seen during May 1952 together with SECR D Class No. 31729. On 20 July 1952 a visit was made to Hayling Island to photograph A1x No. 32655 running round its stock. After leaving school in mid-1953, photographic opportunities were few and far between;

GWR 6400 Class No. 6414 at Plymouth North Road on 7 May 1951.

GWR King Class No. 6017 *King Edward IV* at Newton Abbot with the Down Cornish Riviera Express on 7 September 1952.

GWR 5101 Class No. 5108 is seen on an engineers' train at Newton Abbot on 7 September 1952.

GWR Hall Class No. 6934 *Beachamwell Hall* nears Teignmouth with an Up train on 11 September 1952.

GWR Castle Class No. 7029 *Clun Castle* waits to depart Exeter St David's with the 13.45 Bristol to Penzance on 2 July 1953.

GWR Castle Class No. 5057 *Earl Waldegrave* is captured at Newton Abbot with the 7.30 Paddington to Paignton on 2 July 1953.

SECR H Class No. 31310 stands at Brighton on 27 July 1951.

LBSCR H2 Class No. 32422 *North Foreland* is seen at Brighton in May 1953.

LBSCR A1x No. 32655 running round at Hayling Island on 20 July 1952.

however, after a transfer to Redhill it was possible to photograph L1 Class No. 31756 there on 24 April 1954. The only other photographs from 1954 to survive were taken at Norwich. On 11 December, Brighton and Hove Albion were playing away at Norwich and, as was the custom at that time, a special train ran via New Cross Gate, hauled by one of the H2 Atlantics. This was an ideal opportunity to make a visit to Norwich Thorpe sheds, where among other locomotives D16/3 No. 62510 and K3 No. 61908 were seen.

During my early years working on the Southern Region, I moved round several departments. This was because, like all male employees under the age of eighteen, I was waiting to undertake my National Service and was therefore gaining work experience. By early 1955 I had joined the freight timetable section in the district traffic superintendent's office at Redhill, a hut between the station and engine shed. There I assisted the ballast clerk, who was himself a fine railway photographer and would later provide much encouragement. On 16 April Ian Allan ran a special train from Paddington called 'The Lickley Limited', which I travelled on. The routing was Paddington to Bristol Temple Meads behind Castle Class No. 7017 *G. J. Churchward*, and from Bristol Temple Meads to Bromsgrove behind the same locomotive. From Bromsgrove we were banked up the incline; the formation included the Coronation Beavertail observation car and we were told this vehicle would not be strong enough to take the pressure of being pushed by the banker, No. 58100. Instead, 3F tanks would be used. The train did not have reserved seats so we made our way into the observation car only to find the large locomotive with a big headlamp buffering up; indeed, it was No. 58100, *Big Bertha*, herself. She gave a fine exhaust display before dropping off at the top. A Class 5 took us

SR L1 Class No. 31756 at Redhill on 24 April 1954.

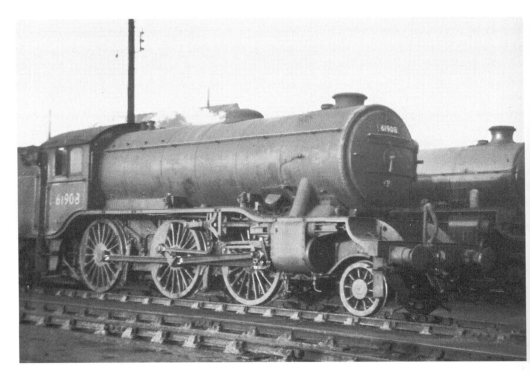

LNER K3 Class No. 61908 is seen at Norwich sheds on 11 December 1954.

from Bromsgrove to New Street, instead of the originally booked Snow Hill, since the Castle was out of gauge over this section. Return to Paddington was behind Castle Class No. 7007 *Great Western*.

There were several inter-regional services passing through Redhill on a daily basis, to and from Birkenhead and Wolverhampton and Eastbourne and Hastings and Kent Coast resorts. Between Redhill and Reading these were usually worked by either Schools Class 4-4-0s, Manor 4-6-0s or GWR Class 43XX 2-6-0s. In May 1955 several BR Standard Class 4 2-6-0s were allocated to Redhill and on 6 May a trial run was made with No. 76054 on the 7.35 Margate to Birkenhead. The trial was successful, although many of the Class 4s only stayed at Redhill for a few months before moving to Eastleigh. On the same day Schools Class No. 30913 *Christ's Hospital* worked the Margate portion of the return working from Birkenhead and the last E Class, No. 31166, worked the Hastings portion. This would prove to be one of No. 31166's last duties since it was withdrawn on the 12th of that month. On 20 May a visit was made to Newport on the Isle of Wight, travelling behind O2 Class W25 *Godshill* from Ryde. At Ryde St John's, W19 *Osborne* was noted stored alongside the sheds. From Newport station the engine shed could be seen containing W3 *Ryde*, W26 *Whitwell*, and W33 *Bembridge*.

Returning to the through services to and from Birkenhead and Wolverhampton, the portion for the Sussex resorts was, until their withdrawal, the province of SECR D Class 4-4-0s. On 17 May No. 31737 worked the Up Hastings portion, on the 19th No. 31734 worked the Down Hastings portion and on 2 September No. 31734 worked the

GWR Castle Class 7017 *G. J. Churchward* leaves Paddington with the 'Lickley Limited' on 16 April 1955. (C. F. Verrall collection, photographer not known)

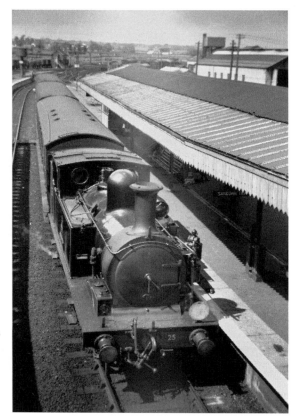

Above: Standard 4 2-6-0 No. 76054 stands at Redhill, waiting to depart with the 7.35 Margate to Birkenhead on 6 May 1955.

Left: LSWR O2 Class W25 *Godshill* is seen at Newport, Isle of Wight, on 10 May 1955.

The Newport, Isle of Wight, sheds. On view are LBSCR E1 Class No. W3 *Ryde*, LSWR O2 Class No. W26 *Whitwell* and LSWR O2 Class No. W33 *Bembridge*. 10 May 1955.

9.25 from Hastings. A friend of mine at Redhill, Pat Farmer, was due to start his National Service so we requested permits to visit Southampton Docks and Eastleigh shed on 8 July. At Southampton we saw a number of USA Tanks, including Nos 30063 and 30067, while on view at Eastleigh was the last D15 Class 4-4-0, No. 30434, King Arthur No. 30449 *Sir Torre*, Urie S15 No. 30509 and BR Standard 3 2-6-2T No. 82012.

As with most years, in 1955 there were many special steam workings seen passing through Wivelsfield. These included U1 Class No. 31897 on a Down special from Birmingham to Eastbourne or Hastings on 22 May; U Class No. 31612 on an Up troop train from the Hastings area, possibly Appledore, on 3 July; Atlantic No. 32421 *South Foreland* with a Down special from Nottingham to Brighton on 3 August; U1 Class No. 31899 from Enfield to Hastings on 31 July; LMS Class 5 No. 45051 on a special from Rugby to Eastbourne on 7 August; and finally N Class No. 31413 on a special from Wellingborough to either Eastbourne or Hastings on 14 August.

Working at Redhill gave me the opportunity to visit the former SECR engine sheds at Tonbridge and Ashford, which I did on 29 July 1955. At Ashford one of the Redhill Standard 4 2-6-0s, No. 76058, was on shed, together with SECR Class C No. 31221, Class E1 No. 31497 and O1 No. 31048. At Tonbridge LCDR R1 0-4-4 tanks No. 31698 and No. 31704 were present, plus LBSCR C2X No. 32438 – this particular locomotive later proved to be the last of the class to be withdrawn and is carrying a boiler with a second dome which originally carried the top-feed. Return to Redhill was behind Schools Class No. 30937 *Epsom*.

SECR D Class No. 31734 enters Wivelsfield with the 9.25 Hastings to Wolverhampton on 2 September 1955.

Standard Class 3 tank No. 82012 at Eastleigh on 8 July 1955.

SECR U Class No. 31612 enters Wivelsfield with an Up troop train from the Hastings area on 3 July 1955.

SECR E1 Class No. 31497 at Ashford on 29 July 1955.

Double-domed LBSCR C2x Class No. 32438, the last of the class, is seen at Tonbridge on 29 July 1955.

SR Schools Class No. 30937 *Epsom* waits to leave Redhill with an Up train on 29 July 1955.

Chapter Two

A Change of Camera: 1955–1959

By early August 1955 I came to the conclusion that the use of a box camera was no longer an option and purchased what I thought would be a more suitable camera, especially with two years of National Service just round the corner. This 'new' camera had three shutter speeds, but since I was ignorant of such things, there were no aperture controls, no means to vary film speeds and fixed focusing. In fact, it turned out to be little more than a glorified three-speed box camera. Early photographs were disappointing to say the least. Sadly, these included a visit to Reading General on 13 August, where among non-usable images of locos I photographed Britannia No. 70022 *Tornado* on the 7.15 Plymouth to Reading, Castle Class No. 5037 *Monmouth Castle* on the 8.19 Kidderminster to Paddington, and many others. I was to find this disappointment was due to technical ignorance. I assumed that to take photographs of moving trains a 'fast' film was needed; however, with a negative just 32 mm by 32 mm, this resulted in excessive grain, or, in modern parlance, 'noise'. This was a lesson quickly learnt, and an example of this is an image taken on 12 August of Standard 4 tank No. 80033, seen leaving Redhill with the 14.07 to Tunbridge Wells West. However, all was not lost as the following day Schools Class No. 30925 *Cheltenham* was successfully photographed passing through Wivelsfield with the 10.15 Victoria to Newhaven Marine boat train.

On the same day I took the short journey to Horsted Keynes to photograph what was believed at the time to be the last train on the Lewes to East Grinstead line. The line was originally due to be closed on 13 June; however, because of an ASLEF strike the last service actually ran on 28 May. A railtour had been organised by the Railway Correspondence & Travel Society, 'The Wealden Limited', which was contracted to run on 12 June. This, of course, had to be cancelled. However, because of the contractual agreement, this tour was rearranged for 14 August, hauled by Atlantic No. 32426 *St Alban's Head*, hence my being at Horsted Keynes. To say there were a lot of people here is an understatement, and one wonders if in fact the electric current of the branch from Ardingly had been turned off. This of course was the start of the battle to reopen the line and the eventual creation of the Bluebell Railway Preservation Society.

Having received my National Service call-up papers in late August, the opportunity was taken to take a visit Tunbridge Wells West from Brighton, using, of course, a much more suitable film stock. While waiting to catch the 8.48 to Tunbridge Wells, hauled by Standard 4 tank No. 80033, the Brighton works shunter, No. 377S, emerged from the stock yard. After walking back down the line from Tunbridge Wells, Standard 4 tank

Left: Standard 4 tank No. 80033 leaves Redhill with 14.07 to Tunbridge Wells West on 12 August 1955.

Below: Schools Class No. 30925 *Cheltenham* leaves Wivelsfield with the 10.15 Victoria to Newhaven Marine boat train on 14 August 1955.

LBSCR H2 Class No. 32426 *St Alban' Head* is captured at Horsted Keynes with the RCTS special 'The Wealden Limited' on 14 August 1955.

LBSCR A1x Class 377S is seen shunting at the Brighton works stock yard on 1 September 1955.

No. 80014 was noted on a service via Oxted, and SECR L Class No. 31765 was seen on a Tonbridge to Brighton service.

After returning home I was able to walk along the public roads to Keymer Junction to see Schools Class No. 30915 *Brighton* pass the signal box with the 17.41 boat train from Newhaven Marine to Victoria. This is now a much changed scene: the signal box and semaphore signals are no more and the footbridge on which I stood has been removed. My parents were on their way to South Devon for their holidays and, as a consequence, on Saturday 3 September I was despatched to spend the weekend with an uncle who lived in Bromley. Waiting to catch my connecting train at London Bridge I photographed Schools Class No. 30934. *St. Lawrence* on a Down Hastings express. Taking the opportunity to do a bit of spotting I remained at Grove Park station and saw at least three Schools Class locos – No. 30902 *Wellington*, No. 30919 *Harrow* and No. 30939 *Leatherhead* – as well as King Arthur No. 30799 *Sir Ironside*. However, the highlight for me was SECR D1 Class No. 31739 on a Down hop-picker special. On the Monday morning I boarded a train to Bedford at St Pancras, thus starting a period when no logs were taken. A few days later I was on a special train that took me to RAF West Kirby, possibly via Bridgnorth, where the RAF had another basic training camp. Sadly I have no details of what motive power was used, nor for when I returned home on a forty-eight-hour pass early in November after completion of basic training. This was on a scheduled service, but I did see the Deltic prototype in Lime Street station that day. My forty-eight-hour pass occurred at the same time as horse racing at Lingfield Park, and gave an opportunity to go to Lingfield, more than likely on a race special, via Ardingly and East Grinstead. Several race specials were

SECR L Class No. 31765 is photographed south of Tunbridge Wells West on 1 September 1955.

Schools Class No. 30915 *Brighton* passes Keymer Junction signal box with the 17.41 boat train from Newhaven Marine to Victoria on 1 September 1955.

Schools Class No. 30934 *St. Lawrence* enters London Bridge Eastern with a Down express on 3 September 1955.

SECR D1 Class No. 31739 is at Grove Park with a Down hop-pickers special on 3 September 1955.

noted, including LMS Class 4 tank No. 42080 on the 11.33 ex-Cannon Street, U1 Class No. 31907 on the 11.30 ex-Victoria and LMS Class 4 tank No. 42100 on the 13.41 ex-East Croydon. Working a scheduled Down service, meanwhile, was Standard 4 tank No. 80031. On my return journey, brand-new Standard 4 tank No. 80127 was seen at Haywards Heath with the Brighton tool vans, attending to the derailed tender of C2x No. 32536. No. 80127 would shortly make the long journey to Corkerhill, where it would remain until withdrawal from service. Shortly afterwards I was again on the move, this time to Worth Matravers (near Swanage) for trade training.

After trade training and Christmas leave I was at a camp in the Birmingham area, where I was given a provisional driving licence, since the unit I was joining was a mobile radar unit and required all personnel to be able to drive. I reported to the military transit office at Liverpool Street to catch a train to Harwich, followed by an overnight voyage on the cattle troop ship to the Hook of Holland and onward to my posting at Goch in Germany – another tortuous journey taking well over twenty-four hours in total. The camp at Goch was not too far from a railway line and, despite having no knowledge of Continental railways, on 22 April I managed to get a photograph of DB No. 56 604 on a freight working. My stay at Goch was relatively short, as it was primarily a transit camp for RAF service personnel on posting to and from Germany, although the unit I was on was based there, and we moved en bloc during May 1956 in a convoy to RAF Schleswig in northern Germany.

Shortly after arriving at RAF Schleswig I returned home on a period of leave. On 15 June Standard Class 4 tank No. 80032 was seen at Wivelsfield while working the

Standard 4 tank No. 80031 enters Lingfield with a Down train on 11 November 1955. Note the stock, including a Pullman car, waiting in the sidings to form a return special.

New Standard 4 tank No. 80127 and the Brighton tool vans attend the re-railing of the tender of C2x No. 32536 at Haywards Heath on 11 November 1955.

Ex-Prussian P8 No. 56 604 is spotted near Goch, North Rhine-Westphalia, with a freight train on 22 April 1956.

17.41 vans from Brighton to London Bridge, while in the opposite direction the prototype 4-CEP units Nos 7101/2/3 worked the 17.48 London Bridge to Brighton. The following day these units were to work the 11.08 semi-fast from Brighton to Victoria. While not a steam working, on the 16th I photographed Co-Co electric locomotive No. 20002 passing through Wivelsfield in the 9.05 Victoria to Newhaven Marine boat train. This and its two sister locomotives were particular favourites of mine and later, in 1963, I was to diagram them to work stone services originating from Meldon Quarry between Chichester and Three Bridges. On 18 June I was at Swindon, possibly having a permit to visit the works and sheds. In the works yard, more than likely acting as a yard pilot, was Taff Vale A Class 382. Withdrawn in April 1956, it was not broken up until September. Also seen alongside the works were 1400 Class No. 1428 and 6400 Class No. 6417, while in the Up bay platform in the station was 5800 Class No. 5804.

On 21 June I went to Salisbury, returning with a stop off at Basingstoke. Of note at Salisbury were the first two rebuilt Merchant Navy Class Pacifics: No. 35018 *British India Line* on the Down Atlantic Coast Express, and No. 35020 *Bibby Line* waiting to undertake a test run. Strangely, all the on-the-road testing was done using No. 35020 rather than No. 35018. On shed were King Arthur No. 30449 *Sir Torre*, County Class No. 1009 *County of Carmarthen* and Lord Nelson No. 30854 *Howard of Effingham*. However, the highlight for me was H15 No. 30332, seen trundling through the station on a freight train. This was a rebuild by Robert Urie of one of the disappointing Drummond Class F13 4-6-0s. My stay at Basingstoke was quite short, but among the workings seen were two Lord Nelson Class 4-6-0s – No. 30857 *Lord Howe* and No. 30865 *Sir John Hawkins* – on Down services via Southampton. On my final day before returning to

Standard 4 tank No. 80032 leaves Wivelsfield with the 17.41 Brighton to London Bridge vans on 14 June 1956.

SR electric locomotive No. 20002 passes through Wivelsfield with the 9.05 Victoria to Newhaven Marine boat train on 16 June 1956.

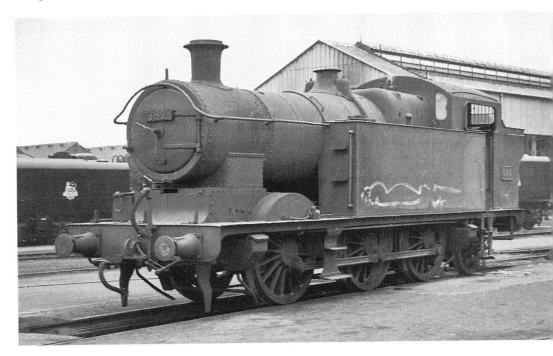

Taff Vale A Class No. 382 is seen in Swindon works yard on 18 June 1956.

GWR 1400 Class No. 1428 and 6400 Class No. 6417 are captured at Swindon on 18 June 1956.

LSWR H15 Class No. 30332, rebuilt from a Class F13, passes through Salisbury station with a Down freight on 21 June 1956.

Germany, on 23 June, I was at Wivelsfield, where N15x No. 32329 *Stephenson* worked a Stephenson Locomotive Society sixty-minute non-stop special from London Bridge to Brighton – back to the pre-electrification days' schedules! Also seen were U1 Class No. 31896 on a special troop train from Stourbridge to Appledore and LMS Class 5 No. 45372 on an excursion from Tring to Brighton. My return to Germany was again via Harwich and the Hook of Holland, this time with an overnight stop at Hamburg.

RAF Schleswig was located just south of the town of Schleswig, itself in Schleswig-Holstein, almost midway between Hamburg and the Danish border. The airfield itself had been established in 1916 and at the end of the Second World War a number of Messerschmitt Me262 jet fighters were based there. While I was stationed at Schleswig, a flight of target towing de Havilland Mosquito aircraft were on station. The town of Schleswig had a local railway system, known as Die Verkehrsbetriebe des Kreises Schleswig (VKS), which was some 105 km in length with a connection at Schleswig with Deutsche Bundesbahn. The VKS had a fleet of Edwardian 0-4-0 and 0-6-0 tank locomotives built by Henschel mainly between 1905 and 1907, although there was a modern 0-6-0 tank named *Dumbo* from 1949. Most of these steam locomotives were used for shunting, but appeared to be out of use, having been replaced by three 0-6-0 diesel-hydraulic locos from MaK and Henschel. I did not actually take a trip on any passenger services, which were worked by 1920s railcars and trailers, the systems being reminiscent of the Kent & East Sussex Railway when Colonel Stephens was in charge. On 6 August 1956 we went on a station outing by coach to Sønderborg (where the Danish Winter Palace is located). I saw a couple of DSB railcars and DSB F Class No. 428, which

LMS Class 5 No. 45372 leaves Wivelsfield with a special from Tring to Brighton on 23 June 1956.

A VKS railcar at Schleswig on 9 March 1957.

VKS 0-4-0 tank No. 9. Built by Henschel in 1907, it is spotted at Schleswig on 14 October 1956.

VKS 0-6-0 tank No. 13. Built by Henschel in 1907, it is awaiting scrapping at Schleswig on 2 February 1957.

VKS 0-6-0 tank No. 21 *Dumbo*. Built by Henschel in 1949, it is also seen in Schleswig on 14 October 1956.

is similar to the Danish locomotive No. 656 on the Nene Valley Railway. I was to take very few photographs on the DB main line at Schleswig, but these included seeing Class V200 diesel-hydraulic No. V200-009 and Class 03 Pacific No. 03-1017 double-heading the 9.05 Nyborg to Hamburg on 20 December 1956. I assume the steam locomotive was there to provide carriage heating, which was something British Railways had to resort to in the winter on 1962/63 when a number of stored and withdrawn locos were brought back into service for that very reason. On 2 February 1957, Class 50 50-1746 was on a northbound freight train. In mid-April 1957 I was back home on my final period of leave. Noted on one day was SECR L Class No. 31771, which was working the 9.24 Hastings to Wolverhampton via Redhill. The L Class locomotives were the last to be designed by H. S. Wainwright. By chance, No. 31771, the last to be built, was one of the final survivors. On 16 April I visited Faversham, where C Class No. 31714 and D1 Class No. 31509 were on shed, while N Class No. 31825 was seen working a local freight service. Later in the day I was to go to Ramsgate; however, no photographs appear to have been taken. I think I must have left the camera at home before returning to Germany, since no images from April 1957 until my demob in late August 1957 have survived.

My National Service finished at the end of August 1957 and I returned to work at Redhill. One of the first things I did was to take some of my accumulated holiday and go back to my old haunts at Teignmouth in South Devon. On 7 September I was at Plymouth and saw Grange Class No. 6813 *Eastbury Grange* outside North Road waiting to back down into the station to act as a pilot on an Up service, this being a

DSB 'F' Class No. 428 is captured at Sønderborg on 6 August 1956.

The DSB Sønderborg shed with a railcar inside, seen on 6 August 1956.

Above: Deutsche Bundsbahn V200 Class No. V200-009 and Deutsche Bundesbahn 03 Class No. 03-1017 are seen near Schleswig with the 9.05 Nyborg to Hamburg on 20 December 1956.

Left: Deutsche Bundesbahn 50 Class No. 50-1746 is seen with a northbound freight on 17 February 1957.

Above: SECR C Class
No. 31714 is at Faversham
on 16 April 1957.

Right: GWR Grange Class
No. 6813 *Eastbury Grange*
is waiting to double-head
an Up train at Plymouth
on 7 September 1957.

regular duty for that class of locomotive. On the same day, Castle Class No. 5006 *Tregenna Castle* worked the 10.20 Plymouth to Paddington and was seen just before going on to the sea wall at Teignmouth. The next day I walked along the sea wall at Teignmouth in time to photograph another Castle, No. 5085 *Evesham Abbey,* leaving Parson's Tunnel with a Kingswear-bound special train. Also seen in the Teignmouth area were 5101 Class No. 4176 on the 11.05 Exeter St David's to Newton Abbot, Modified Hall Class No. 7901 *Dodington Hall* on a Down train and Hall Class No. 5904 *Kelham Hall* also on a Down service. On the 10th I was at Exeter St David's, where I saw 5101 Class No. 4174, which was working the 14.15 to Torquay, and Grange Class 6874 *Haughton Grange,* which was shunting passenger stock. My final day in South Devon, on 10 September, was again spent on the Teignmouth sea wall. Seen that day were GWR Castle Class No. 4086 *Builth Castle* on what was possibly the 5.30 Paddington to Penzance, GWR 5101 Class No. 4176 on the 11.00 Exeter St David's to Newton Abbot, GWR Grange Class No. 6856 *Stowe Grange* on an Up service to Manchester and 43XX Class No. 5336 on an Up freight.

GWR Castle Class No. 5006 *Tregenna Castle* leaves Teignmouth with the 10.20 Plymouth to Paddington on 7 September 1957.

GWR Castle Class No. 5085 *Evesham Abbey* leaves Parson's Tunnel with a Down special to Kingswear on 8 September 1957.

GWR Grange Class No. 6874 *Haughton Grange* shunts stock at Exeter St David's on 10 September 1957.

GWR 43XX Class No. 5336
is spotted near Teignmouth
with an Up freight
on 10 September 1957.

After that it was back to Redhill to resume working in the freight section. On
11 November 1957 I made a trip to Eastleigh sheds. Seen working were Urie Class S15
No. 30507 on a freight from Feltham or Basingstoke, Urie H15 No. 30334, which was a
rebuild of a Drummond Class F13, and Standard 3 tank No. 82015 on a short freight to
Fawley. The Class 3s worked these services until they became too heavy, at which point
they were replaced by Urie Class H16 tanks. These in turn were replaced by the large
Maunsell Class W tanks. Urie Class S15 No. 30509 was seen moving several ex-works
locos, including LMS Class 2 tank No. 41292 and King Arthur Class No. 30796
Sir Dodinas le savage. On shed was another King Arthur, No. 30782 *Sir Brian*, as well
as BR Standard 5 No. 73113, later to be named *Lyonesse,* and LMS 8F No. 48775.
This last locomotive had recently been purchased from the War Department, where it
was numbered 512, and it had been overhauled at Eastleigh. On one misty December
day in 1957 I had taken my camera to work and saw Schools Class No. 30917
Ardingly come past the sheds with a service from Tonbridge. In the reverse direction
SECR L Class No. 31767 was on its way to Tonbridge. I was just able to make a single
photographic outing in 1958, which took place on 25 January. This was a rewarding
trip, and I saw among others SECR L Class No. 31777, one of the German-built locos

Ex-works SR King Arthur Class No. 30796 *Sir Dodinas le savage* is seen at Eastleigh sheds on 9 November 1957.

BR Standard Class 3 tank No. 82015 leaves Eastleigh with a freight to Fawley on 9 November 1957.

Ex-works after purchase from the War Department, LMS Class 8F No. 48775 is also seen at Eastleigh on 9 November 1957

SECR L Class No. 31767 passes Redhill shed with a service to Tonbridge in December 1957.

on the 13.05 Redhill to Tunbridge Wells West; Schools Class No. 30910 *Merchant Taylors* leaving on a Down Hastings service; Schools Class No. 30920 *Rugby* on an Up train; Merchant Navy Class No. 35001 *Channel Packet* on an Up boat train; Q1 Class No. 33028 and C Class No. 31270 on freight workings; and finally L1 Class No. 31787 double-heading L Class No. 31781 on a Down boat train. These were in fact the last photographs that I would take with that camera. I was far from satisfied with its performance and was not in a position to replace it. In addition, I was finding it difficult to devote the time at weekends to go travelling far; that is not to say I had lost interest in railway locomotives, quite the reverse. Since working at Redhill I was able keep myself aware of locomotive movement and, sadly, withdrawals.

SR Schools Class No. 30910 *Merchant Taylors* leaves Tonbridge with a Hastings service on 25 January 1958.

SR Merchant Navy Class No. 35001 *Channel Packet* passes through Tonbridge with an Up boat train on 25 January 1958.

SR L1 Class No. 31787 double-heads SECR L Class No. 31781 on a Down boat train at Tonbridge on 25 January 1958.

Chapter Three

A Newer Camera and Back Taking Photographs: 1961

By August 1961 I had become concerned with the reduction in the number of steam-hauled services, especially in the London area, and, with the encouragement of some of the photographers working at Redhill, I decided that I should get a decent camera and record some of what was still in operation. Of course, most of the suburban services had either been replaced by DEMUs, an extension of existing electrification or Type 2 diesel locomotives. In addition the Kent Coast electrification scheme had been completed. I therefore purchased a second-hand twin-lens reflex camera, similar to a Rolleiflex. Why I bought a TLR rather than a Rangefinder camera I cannot recall, but after my experience with the recently discarded camera I was loathe at that time to consider a 35-mm camera. The next decision was where to go, mainly at weekends and within a reasonably striking distance from my home by Wivelsfield station or from Redhill. Taking advice, I obtained lineside permits for the Eastern Region from Finsbury Park to Hitchin, and for the Midland Region north of the end of the Watford electrification, also in the Kettering area. I still had my old non-electrified areas permit for the Southern Region, and for some reason did not get a permit for the Western Region. No high-vis jackets in those days, or having to pay to go on awareness course; in my mind if you could not see or hear approaching trains, then there was something wrong. In any case, you must never put yourself in a dangerous position.

My first foray with the new camera was to Brighton on 12 August, where, on shed, were LBSCR K Class No. 32347, LMS Class 2 tank No. 41303 and Battle of Britain Class No. 34083 *605 Squadron*. Meanwhile, Standard 4 tank No. 80138 worked the 15.30 to Horsham via Steyning, usually rostered for a LMS Class 2 tank duty. Eager to use the camera, on 14 August I took a lunchtime trip to East Croydon to photograph LMS Class 5 No. 44830 on the 9.30 'Leicester Holiday Express' from Leicester to Brighton. Interestingly, I have subsequently found that that same locomotive and headboard combination had been seen at other destinations around that time, and indeed the headboard, or one remarkably similar, was used on the Great Central Railway in 2017. On 17 August I walked along the cinder path from my office to the rear of Redhill loco shed, where SECR U Class No. 31616, SECR N Class No. 31868 and Schools Class No. 30924 *Haileybury* were outside. A short trip to Harrow and Wealdstone on the 18th found LMS Class 5 No. 45004 on a Down train, as well as Derby Type 2 diesel D5036. English Electric Type 4 diesel D328 was on an Up express, as was LMS rebuilt Jubilee Class No. 45736 *Phoenix*. No. 45736 was one of two Jubilee Class locomotive to be

Standard Class 4
tank No. 80138
leaves Brighton with
the 15.30 Brighton
to Horsham
via Steyning
on 12 August 1961.

Brighton shed as seen from Platform 1 of Brighton station. From the left there is a LBSCR E6 Class
on coaling stage duties, a Standard Class 4 tank, a Bulleid Pacific (possibly No. 34083), a LBSCR
A1x and two LBSCR K Class locomotives. 12 August 1961.

LMS Class 5 No. 44830 is at East Croydon with the 9.30 Leicester to Brighton Holiday Express on 14 August 1961.

The rear of Redhill shed, showing SECR U Class No. 31612, SECR N Class No. 31868 and Schools Class No. 30924 *Haileybury*. 17 August 1961.

fitted with a larger boiler and double chimney similar to that later used on the rebuilt Royal Scot Class locomotives. Sunday 20 August led to diesel-hauled excursion specials coming to Brighton from Leagrave and Broxbourne; however, Battle of Britain Class No. 34083 *605 Squadron* worked the 9.06 excursion from High Wycombe. Nominally an Ashford engine, No. 34083 had been displaced following completion of the Kent Coast Electrification, and was probably working from Stewarts Lane before being reallocated to Exmouth Junction in November.

On 2 September I took a trip to Reading General. The station pilot was an immaculate GWR Hall Class No. 6913 *Levens Hall*. How this name came to be used must be one of Paddington's mysteries, since this Hall is in Cumbria. Seen working were GWR Castle Class No. 5096 *Bridgwater Castle* on the 13.50 Paddington to Neyland, GWR 43XX Class No. 6313 on the 10.42 Wolverhampton to Ramsgate (which it would work as far as Redhill) and GWR Hall Class No. 6937 *Conyngham Hall* on the 14.40 to Swindon. Warship D817 *Foxhound* headed the 10.35 Torquay to Paddington. A visit was made to the loco sheds, where GWR 5700 Class No. 4661, GWR 6100 Class No. 6163, GWR 7200 Class No. 7238, WD 2-8-0 No. 90315 and Standard Class 9 No. 92207 were seen, among others. The only thing of interest during a short visit to Brighton on 9 September was the sight of SR Q Class No. 30544 running about with the smoke box door wide open. What effect that had on the fire is left to the imagination.

Rebuilt LMS Patriot Class No. 45736 *Phoenix* passes through Harrow & Wealdstone with an Up express on August 19 1961.

SR Battle of Britain Class No. 34083 *605 Squadron* leaves Wivelsfield with the 9.06 High Wycombe to Brighton excursion on 20 August 1961.

GWR Castle Class No. 5096 *Bridgwater Castle* leaves Reading General with the 13.50 Paddington to Neyland on 2 September 1961.

GWR 43XX Class No. 6313 enters Reading General with the 10.42 Wolverhampton to Ramsgate on 2 September 1961.

GWR 7200 Class No. 7238 is seen on Reading shed on 2 September 1961.

WD Class 2-8-0 No. 90315 is also seen on Reading shed on 2 September 1961.

SR Q Class No. 30544 at Brighton 9 September 1961.

On 15 September I was in Edinburgh armed with permits for Dalry Road, Haymarket and St Margarets sheds. I think the original objective was to see the remaining Large Director and North British 4-4-0s. However, I was out of luck, as all had been withdrawn or were in store elsewhere. In any case the weather was pretty foul and not conducive to photography. All was not lost however, as at Haymarket LNER A2/3 No. 60519 *Honeyway* was being shunted, while LNER (ex-NBR) J83 0-6-0 tank No. 68481 was found outside one of the sheds. Being prepared for the Up 'Queen of the Scots' was English Electric Type 4 diesel D348. At St Margarets a scruffy LNER B1 Class, No. 61099, was being prepared, complete with circular headboard, to work a National Trust for Scotland Rhum Special, and the roundhouse shunter, LNER ex-NBR Y9 Class No. 68095, was seen standing outside. Finally, at Dalry Road, LNER (ex-NBR) Class J37 No. 64554 was out of use in a siding, as was CR 652 Class No. 57634. However, CR Class 812 No. 57550 was in steam.

Shortly afterwards the offices at Redhill were moved to the newly completed Essex House office block adjacent to East Croydon station to form part of the newly created central section divisional manager's office. My last photographs taken at Redhill were from the top of the coal dump at the rear of the sheds and were of Standard 4 tank No. 80059 working the 11.05 Redhill to Tonbridge on 27 September and the 15.12 Redhill to Tonbridge on 29 October. Now working at East Croydon I was able to photograph SECR N Class No. 31410 leaving on the reversible line with the 11.54 race special from Victoria to Lingfield on 4 October. By now I had received my trackside

LNER A2/3 No. 60519 *Honeyway* is captured at Haymarket shed on 15 September 1961.

LNER J83 No. 68481 is also seen at Haymarket shed on 15 September 1961.

CR 812 Class No. 57550 stands at Dalry Road shed on 15 September 1961.

Standard Class 4 tank No. 80059 leaves Redhill with the 11.05 to Tonbridge on 27 September 1961.

SECR N Class No. 31410 leaves East Croydon on the reversible line with the 11.54 Race Special from Victoria to Lingfield on 4 October 1961.

permit for the Eastern Region lines south of Hitchin, and on 7 October I was at Hitchin to catch LNER V2 Class No. 60903 heading the 1.00 Class 4 freight Inverkeithing to King's Cross. For some reason, this was the only photograph from that date to survive. On 14 October I caught the 9.40 Brighton to Bournemouth West, hauled by SR West Country Class No. 34019 *Bideford,* as far as Bournemouth Central. This was a service that was to be discontinued with the introduction of the 1962 winter timetable. While at Bournemouth I made a quick visit to the engine sheds before retracing my steps back to Eastleigh. At Eastleigh a number of withdrawn locos were on shed awaiting their fate, including Lord Nelson Class No. 30858 *Lord Duncan,* Class M7s Nos 30668 and 30044, SECR D1 Class No. 31145 and LSWR Adams tank No. 30584. Also on shed was a recent arrival from Rhyl, LMS Class 2 tank No. 41216, which was waiting to go into Eastleigh works for onward transfer to Barnstaple Junction. Lastly, working the 14.44 empty stock to Southampton was Standard 4 4-6-0 No. 75077. A visit was made on 27 October to Aston and Saltley sheds. At Aston, LMS Class 5 No. 45052 was seen being turned and, although not a steam working, Metro-Cammell railcar No. 50313 was worth photographing on a local service.

Basingstoke was visited on 4 November, with few photographs taken, however Schools Class No. 30905 *Tonbridge* worked an Up freight working, this particular

Double-chimney LNER V2 Class No. 60903 enters Hitchin on the 1.00 Inverkeithing to King's Cross express freight on 7 October 1961.

West Country Class No. 34019 *Bideford* leaves Bournemouth Central with the 9.30 Brighton to Bournemouth West on 14 October 1961.

On shed at Bournemouth are LSWR S15 Class No. 30513, rebuilt Battle of Britain Class No. 34056 *Croydon*, Merchant Navy Class No. 35024 *East Asiatic Company*, rebuilt West Country Class No. 34039 *Boscastle* and Standard 4 2-6-0 No. 76027. 14 October 1961.

LSWR Adams tank No. 30584 is seen at Eastleigh, waiting to be scrapped, on 14 October 1961.

SECR E1 Class No. 31145 is also waiting to be scrapped at Eastleigh on 14 October 1961.

LMS Class 2 tank No. 41216, waiting to go into the works at Eastleigh on 14 October 1961.

Standard 4 4-6-0 No. 75077 leaves Eastleigh with the 14.44 empty stock to Southampton on 14 October 1961.

LMS Class 5 No. 45052 on Aston turntable on 27 October 1961.

Diesel unit M50313 passes Aston sheds on 27 October 1961.

engine had been fitted with the self-weighing tender previously used by No. 30933 *Blundells;* en route from Bletchley to Eastleigh works was LMS Class 2 tank No. 41275 One of my duties as ballast clerk at Essex House was to make a weekly visit to the district engineer's office at Purley, the timing of these visits sometime coincided with the departure of the 12.08 freight to Tattenham Corner, and on 6 November this working was headed by LBSCR K Class No. 32346. One of the last visits I made in 1961 was to Salisbury, on 25 November. Several services to and from the Western Region were observed, the most notable being a freight worked by GWR 4700 Class 4702 – a rare sight indeed. Also seen were Merchant Navy Class No. 35029 Ellerman Lines on the Down Atlantic Coast Express, and GWR Hall Class No. 6936 *Breccles Hall*, which worked the 9.30 Portsmouth to Cardiff. The station pilot was the newly transferred from Exmouth Junction LSWR M7 Class No. 30021.

Schools Class No. 30905 *Tonbridge* is seen near Basingstoke with an Up freight on 4 November 1961.

LBSCR K Class No. 32346 leaves Purley with the 12.08 freight to Tattenham Corner on 6 November 1961.

GWR 4700 Class No. 4702 enters Salisbury with a freight service on 25 November 1961.

Merchant Navy Class No. 35029 *Ellerman Lines* leaves Salisbury with the Down Atlantic Coast Express on 25 November 1961.

Chapter Four

An Almost Full
Photographic Year: 1962

The procedure on the Southern Region was for loco-hauled coaching stock requiring to go to Lancing works for attention to be sent to Eardley Sidings in South London, and a conditional 12.23 service to be run when required. The 12.23 was run on 9 January when it was hauled by Schools Class No. 30929 *Malvern* and on 10 January when the motive power was U Class No. 31614 – in both instances photographs were taken at East Croydon. My first visit in 1962 was on 13 January to a cold Reading General. The stay was relatively short, but I was able to see GWR King Class 6000 *King George V* in the station with the 4.55 Fishguard to Paddington, GWR Castle Class 5073 *Blenheim* worked the 6.25 Swansea to Paddington; in addition Warship diesels D821 *Greyhound* and D823 *Hermes* were on the 8.50 Worcester to Paddington and the 9.30 Plymouth to Paddington respectively

The weather at Hitchin on 31 January was gloomy, LNER A3 No. 60062 *Minoru*, leaking steam everywhere, worked what I had noted was the 12.57 Peterborough to King's Cross and sister engine No. 60044 *Melton* headed the 13.15 King's Cross to Peterborough, a regular A3 turn; LNER A1 Class No. 60136 *Alcazar* kept the spotters busy with the 14.40 King's Cross to York.

One of the advantages in working in the office at Essex House was the ability to see workings on the main line. On 2 February I took advantage of this to photograph K Class No. 32343 on the 8.43 freight from Three Bridges to Norwood (note the collection of cars parked below). From a similar viewpoint Dukedog No. 9017 was seen on the 10th on its way to the Bluebell Railway, although sadly no photograph of mine appears to have survived. 9 February saw my first visit of the year to Eastleigh, and one of the advantages of having a lineside pass was the ability to access the sheds from the trackside. As on my previous visit, several withdrawn locos were present, including LSWR Adams Tank No. 30582, Lord Nelson No. 30864 *Sir Martin Frobisher*, Schools Class No. 30927 *Clifton* and SECR C Class No. 31723. There were several other locos of interest on shed, including a pair of LMS Class 2 tanks, Nos 41293 and 41311, with different chimneys, Bristol Barrow Road Standard Class 9 No. 92006 and ex-works 5700 Class No. 7782. Modified West Country Class No. 34016 *Bodmin* left with the 14.00 to Bournemouth and fellow modified West Country No. 34025 *Whimple* passed by on the 11.30 Waterloo to Weymouth, as did West Country No. 34039 *Boscastle*, which was working the 9.17 Weymouth to Waterloo. What must have been a lunchtime visit to Redhill on the 11th saw SECR N Class No. 31854 under the coal stage. A visitor was SECR H Class No. 31005,

Schools Class No. 30930 *Malvern* leaves East Croydon with the 12.23 Eardley Sidings to Lancing works empty stock on 9 January 1962.

This time U Class No. 31614 is seen at East Croydon with the 12.23 Eardley Sidings to Lancing works empty stock on 10 January 1962.

GWR Castle Class No. 5073 *Blenheim* is seen entering Reading General with the 6.25 Swansea to Paddington on 13 January 1962.

LNER A3 No. 60062 *Minoru* leaves Hitchin with the 12.57 Peterborough to King's Cross on 31 January 1962.

K Class No. 32343 enters East Croydon with the 8.43 Three Bridges to Norwood freight on 2 February 1962.

LSWR Adams tank No. 30582 awaits scrapping at Eastleigh on 9 February 1962.

Lord Nelson Class No. 30864 *Sir Martin Frobisher* is spotted at Eastleigh on 9 February 1962.

SECR C Class No. 31723 is also at Eastleigh on 9 February 1962.

LMS Class 2 tank No. 41293 stands at Eastleigh on 9 February 1962.

Also seen at Eastleigh on 9 February 1962 is LMS Class 2 tank No. 41311.

Modified West Country No. 34025 *Whimple* passes Eastleigh shed entrance on the 11.30 Waterloo to Weymouth on 9 February 1962.

Ex-works 5700 Class No. 7782 is spotted at Eastleigh on 9 February 1962.

which was possibly in for some minor repairs, and at the back of the shed Schools Class No. 30916 *Whitgift* stood in front of an ancient coach of unknown origin.

My first visit in March was on the 10th to Basingstoke, and the weather left a lot to be desired. However, I walked down to the flyover at Battledown, where the Waterloo to the West of England lines go beneath those to Southampton and Bournemouth, to catch modified West Country Class No. 34004 *Yeovil* working the 10.54 Waterloo to Salisbury.

From a photographic point of view my visit to Scotland on 16 March, was a disaster; there was something wrong with the film winder and I only ended up with three usable images. One was of Standard Class No. 73105 at Eastfield and another was of Caprotti Standard No. 73149 at St Rollox. What was really frustrating was the loss of a series of trains seen climbing out from Perth station. I had actually made my way as far as Boat of Garten to see the locomotive stored for potential preservation, HR Small Ben No. 54398 *Ben Alder*. When I was there the shed staff expressed their surprise since not that many people had made the pilgrimage to see it. In 1966 the decision was made not to preserve this little loco, with the attitude being, 'Well you already have the Jones Goods No. 103, why do you want another Highland engine?' The same attitude was to apply earlier when there were plans to add SECR L1 Class No. 31757 to the list of locomotives in the National Collection; the attitude was 'You already have LSWR T9 No. 120', despite the fact the L1 was the last traditional British inside-cylinder 4-4-0 in working condition.

A visit to Hitchin on 31 March was much more rewarding. Among the services seen were the 11.50 Harrogate to King's Cross hauled by LNER A4 No. 60013 *Dominion of*

SECR N Class No. 31854 is photographed at Redhill coaling plant on 11 February 1962.

Schools Class No. 30916 *Whitgift* is captured alongside Redhill shed on 11 February 1962.

H Class No. 31005 is captured at Redhill shed on 11 February 1962.

Modified West Country
No. 34004 *Yeovil* is
spotted at Battledown
with the 10.54 Waterloo
to Salisbury on
10 March 1962.

Standard Class 5 No. 73105 is seen at Eastfield on 16 March 1962.

Standard Class 5 No. 73149 is fitted with a Caprotti valve gear at St Rollox on 16 March 1962.

New Zealand, the 14.00 King's Cross to Newcastle with LNER A3 No. 60056 *Centenary* and the 1.00 Inverkeithing to King's Cross, which was hauled by double-chimney LNER V2 No. 60862. Another V2, No. 60874, was in a Down freight, while Standard 9 No. 92181 was stopped in the sheds awaiting repair – a good visit indeed!

On 1 April, of all days, the restored GNR J52/2 Class 1247 worked the 'Blue Belle' special from London Bridge to Sheffield Park via Haywards Heath. It was seen leaving East Croydon, and the building in the background is the divisional manager's Essex House offices. A return to Harrow and Wealdstone was made on 19 April, when several steam workings were noted, including rebuilt Royal Scot No. 46136 *The Border Regiment* on the 13.55 Euston to Liverpool, Patriot No. 45624 *Helena* on an Up freight, LMS Class 5s Nos 45198 and 45128 on a Down express freight, Class 5 No. 45256 on an Up extra working and LMS Class 8F No. 48635 on an Up freight. I think it is important to say here that I would often spend quite a short period of time at places where I was taking photographs.

On the 21st I was again at Salisbury, where the light could have been a lot better. A working of note was GWR 7200 Class No. 7205 on a freight train and Merchant Navy Class No. 35001 *Channel Packet*, which was in charge of the Down Atlantic Coast Express. On the 22nd a quick visit to Three Bridges found LSWR M7 Class No. 30053 in the Up local line platform, taking water between working auto train services to Tunbridge Well West via East Grinstead High Level. Later that day LMS Class 5s Nos 44896 and 44945 worked the 9.15 excursion from Bedford to Brighton and the 8.35 excursion from Leicester to Brighton respectively.

LNER V2 Class No. 60862 leaves Hitchin with the 1.00 Inverkeithing to King's Cross express freight on 31 March 1962.

Standard Class 9 No. 92181 awaits repairs at Hitchin on 31 March 1962.

Restored GNR Class J52/2 No. 1247 leaves East Croydon with the 'Blue Belle' special, London Bridge to Sheffield Park, on 1 April 1962.

Rebuilt Royal Scot No. 46136 *The Border Regiment* is seen at Harrow & Wealdstone with the 13.55 Euston to Liverpool on 19 April 1962.

LMS Class 5s Nos 45198 and 45128 are also seen at Harrow & Wealdstone on 19 April 1962, this time with a Down express freight.

Merchant Navy Class No. 35001 *Channel Packet* is spotted near Wilton with the Down Atlantic Coast Express on 21 April 1962.

LSWR M7 Class No. 30053 takes water at Three Bridges on 22 April 1962.

On 5 May I was at Redhill to see the interesting working of LSWR 700 Class No. 30698 hauling Schools Class No. 30906 *Sherborne* to Ashford. Strangely, No. 30906 was to return to traffic and to survive until the end of 1962, whereas No. 30698 was withdrawn later in May. I then went to a damp Gomshall, on the Redhill to Guildford line, to see SECR N Class No. 31866 on the 9.34 freight from Hoo Junction to Reading and Schools Class No. 30930 *Radley* with the 10.50 Wolverhampton to Ramsgate – a regular Schools turn. Again the weather at Hitchin on 12 May was miserable. It was Rugby League Cup Final day and LNER A1 Class No. 60121 *Silurian* worked an Up special. There were also several other steam workings to be seen, including A4 No. 60006 *Sir Ralph Wedgwood* on the 10.25 King's Cross to Grantham, V2 No. 60880 on the 10.45 King's Cross to Newcastle, V2 No. 60872 *King's Own Yorkshire Light Infantry* on the 11.30 King's Cross to Aberdeen and Standard Class 9 No. 92148 on the 9.50 freight from Ferme Park to New England. Two Baby Deltics, D5907 and D5908, were also seen working freight services. The weather was kinder on the 19th for a quick visit to Wood Green and New Southgate, where I spotted A3 Class No. 60067 *Ladas* on the 7.15 Halifax to King's Cross, WD 2-8-0 No. 90664 and Class 9s Nos 92040 and 92143, which were working freights.

A return visit to Eastleigh was made on 2 June. Several Bulleid Pacifics were on shed, rebuilt West Country No. 34022 *Exmoor* worked the 14.00 to Bournemouth and Merchant Navy Class No. 35017 *Belgian Marine* worked the 11.30 Waterloo to Weymouth. Lord Nelson Class No. 30862 *Lord Collinwood* was seen coming onto shed,

700 Class No. 30698 is seen at Redhill, hauling Schools Class No. 30906 *Sherborne* en route to Ashford on 5 May 1962.

N Class No. 31866 is seen at Westcott with the 9.34 Hoo Junction to Reading freight on 5 May 1962.

Schools Class
No. 30916 *Whitgift*
climbs Gomshall
bank with the 10.50
Wolverhampton
to Ramsgate
on 5 May 1962.

A1 No. 60121 *Silurian* is seen south of Hitchin with a Rugby League special from Halifax to Wembley on 12 May 1962.

Left: Class 9 No. 92148 is spotted south of Hitchin with the 9.50 Ferme Park to New England freight on 12 May 1962.

Below: Class 9 No. 92143 is captured at Wood Green with a Down cement train on 19 May 1962.

while at the rear of the works withdrawn O2 Class No. 30193 was acting as a stationary boiler. On the following day I made my way to Birchden Junction to photograph K Class No. 32349 working a weed-killing train consisting of withdrawn tenders. That evening I was to catch an overnight train to Exeter. Before taking any photographs in the Exeter area, a visit was made to Plymouth Laira shed, where Castle Class 4087 *Cardigan Castle* was seen, recently withdrawn 4500 Class No. 4566 was in the roundhouse and several others were positioned by the turntable. Most of the passenger services were diesel-hauled, mainly by Warships, although D600 *Active* was waiting to leave North Road with the Up Cornish Rivera Express. Outside the new Laira diesel depot were Warship D854 *Tiger* and Type 2 D6305, while Warship D846 *Steadfast* worked the 10.30 to Paddington. Returning to Exeter St David's, light Pacifics Nos 34002 *Salisbury* and 34076 *41 Squadron* worked portions of the Down Atlantic Coast Express, while 1400 Class No. 1466 worked the 14.08 to Brampton.

On the 5th I concentrated on the Exeter area. All the locos seen of the GWR shed were kept clean, including the withdrawn 5400 Class No. 5412, modified Hall No. 6965 *Thirlestaine Hall* and 43XX Class No. 7341. Z Class Nos 30956 and 30950 banked the 13.55 stone train from Meldon Quarry up the incline between the two main Exeter stations. At Exmouth Junction shed, several Bulleid Pacifics were present, including Nos 34035 *Shaftesbury*, 34074 *46 Squadron*, 34076 *41 Squadron*, 34106 *Lydford* and 34107 *Blandford Forum*. Merchant Navy No. 35012 *United States Lines* passed with the Up Atlantic Coast Express; also passing was Standard Class 3 tank No. 82022

Merchant Navy No. 35017 *Belgian Marine* is seen nearing Eastleigh with the 11.30 Waterloo to Weymouth on 2 June 1962.

Lord Nelson No. 30862
Lord Collingwood
enters Eastleigh sheds
on 2 June 1962.

Modified West Country No. 34022 *Exmoor* leaves Eastleigh with the 14.00 to Bournemouth on 2 June 1962.

K Class No. 32349 is seen near Birchden Junction with a weed-killing train on 3 June 1962.

Castle Class No. 4087 *Cardigan Castle* is captured on Plymouth Laira shed on 4 June 1962.

Plymouth Laira shed roundhouse with an unknown 43XX Class, Castle Class No. 7022 *Hereford Castle*, 4575 Class Nos 5544 and 5564, and 6400 Class No. 6438. 4 June 1962.

1400 Class No. 1466 leaves Exeter St David's with the 14.08 to Bampton on 4 June 1962.

GWR 43XX Class No. 7341 stands at Exeter shed on 4 June 1962.

GWR 5400 Class No. 5412 is seen stored at Exeter shed on 5 June 1956, after having been withdrawn the previous April.

Z Class Nos 30956 and 30950 are seen between Exeter St David's and Exeter Central, banking the 11.55 ex-Meldon Quarry on 5 June 1962.

on the 12.15 Exeter Central to Exmouth, while shunting in the goods sidings was Z Class No. 30957. Finally, on the 6th I went to Okehampton and the quarry at Meldon. At Okehampton an unusual sight was rebuilt West Country No. 34096 *Trevone* on the 11.51 Exeter to Plymouth. The rebuilds normally did not work west of Exeter since they were restricted to the main line only.

On the 13th I was back in Scotland, this time at Dundee and Thornton sheds. At Tay Bridge B1 No. 61340 and J37 No. 64587 were among others on shed, while at Thornton Class 5 No. 44784, B1 No. 61330, J37 No. 64636, N15/1 No. 69204 and WD 2-8-0 No. 90350 were seen. On the 15th I was on my way to Wood Green, and at King's Cross Britannia Class No. 70039 *Sir Christopher Wren* was waiting to work a service to Cleethorpes. Then, at Wood Green several A4s were seen, including No. 60006 *Sir Ralph Wedgwood* on a Down special from Leeds, No. 60008 *Dwight D. Eisenhower* on an Up troop special, No. 60015 *Quicksilver* on the 15.20 King's Cross to Leeds and No. 60019 *Bittern* on the 13.05 freight from King's Cross to Edinburgh. Other Pacifics seen were Nos 60062 *Minoru*, 60109 *Hermit*, 60122 *Curlew* and 60132 *Marmion*. Standard 9 No. 92038 worked an Up freight service and not to be forgotten were the Deltics, a favourite of mine and others just for their size, sheer power and sound. D9007 *Pinza* impressed with the 13.00 King's Cross to Edinburgh.

Merchant Navy No. 35012 *United States Lines* nears Exmouth Junction with the Up Atlantic Coast Express on 5 June 1962.

Modified West Country No. 34096 *Trevone* is seen at Okehampton with the 11.51 Exeter to Plymouth on 6 June 1962.

B1 No. 61340 is spotted at Dundee Tay Bridge on 13 June 1962.

J37 No. 64636 is seen at Thornton Junction on 13 June 1962.

N15/1 No. 69204 is at Thornton Junction on 13 June 1962.

WD 2-8-0 No. 90350 is seen at Thornton Junction on 6 March 1962.

Britannia No. 70039 *Sir Christopher Wren* is captured at King's Cross on 15 June 1962.

A4 No. 60015 *Quicksilver* is seen at Wood Green with the 15.20 King's Cross to Leeds on 15 June 1962.

A4 No. 60019 *Bittern* is seen at Wood Green with the 13.05 King's Cross to Aberdeen freight on 15 June 1962.

Class 9 No. 92038 is spotted at Wood Green with an Up freight on 15 June 1962.

Deltic D9007 *Pinza* is seen at Wood Green with the 13.00 King's Cross to Edinburgh on 15 June 1962.

A visit to Farnborough Hants was made on the 23rd. Most of the main line workings were hauled by Bulleid Pacifics; however, a Down empty stock working was hauled by King Arthur No. 30765 *Sir Gareth*, and on the Reading to Guildford lines Manor No. 7808 *Cookham Manor* worked the 10.35 Birkenhead to Hastings. On the 24th the Locomotive Club of Great Britain ran 'The Sussex Coast Limited Rail Tour' using T9 No. 120, M7 No. 30055, K Class No. 32353, E4 No. 32503 and E6 No. 32417. I was to see No. 120 entering Christ's Hospital from Guildford and No. 32353 near Arundel. On the way to Christ's Hospital, H Class No. 31522 was sitting in the bay platform at Three Bridges, waiting to work a service to Tunbridge Wells West. I was working on the morning of the 30th and therefore decided to catch the 12.42 Waterloo to Basingstoke, which was hauled by the restored T9 No. 120 – a duty it was also to undertake the following Saturday. It was good to see families in their back gardens waving to the old girl as we went past. Of particular interest at Basingstoke were King Arthur No. 30793 *Sir Onzlake* on the 12.38 Portsmouth to Birmingham and Lord Nelson No. 30856 *Lord St Vincent* on the 13.11 Portsmouth to Birmingham.

July started with another visit to Ferme Park and Haringay West on the 7th. A4 No. 60001 *Sir Ronald Matthews* was seen working the 14.55 freight from King's Cross to Niddie, while A4 No. 60003 *Andrew K. McCosh* worked the 09.20 Sunderland to King's Cross and No. 60030 *Golden Fleece* worked the 13.52 King's Cross to Peterborough. Other LNER Pacifics seen included A3s Nos 60073 *St Gatien* and 60105 *Victor Wild*, while A1s Nos 60122 *Curlew* and 60148 *Aboyeur* also made an appearance. B1 No. 61073 was on the 14.15 King's Cross to Cleethorpes and Britannia No. 70038 *Robin Hood* headed the 7.43 Cleethorpes to Kings' Cross. Lastly, the Brush Type 4 prototype D0280 *Falcon* was seen on the 15.15 King's Cross to Sheffield.

King Arthur No. 30765 *Sir Gareth* is seen near Farnborough with a Down empty stock train on 23 June 1962.

Manor Class 7808 *Cookham Manor* is about to pass beneath the Waterloo to the West of England lines with the 10.35 Birmingham to Hastings on 23 June 1962.

T9 No. 120 approaches Christ's Hospital with the Sussex Coast Limited Rail Tour on 24 June 1962.

K Class No. 32353 is seen near Arundel with the Sussex Coast Limited Rail Tour, 24 June 1962.

Right: H Class
No. 31522 stands
at Three Bridges
on 24 June 1962.

Below: Restored
T9 No. 120 rests at
Basingstoke shed after
working the 12.42
from Waterloo on
30 June 1962.

A4 No. 60001 *Sir Ronald Matthews* is captured near Ferme Park with the 14.55 King's Cross to Edinburgh freight on 7 July 1962.

A4 No. 60030 *Golden Fleece* is seen near Ferme Park on the 13.52 King's Cross to Peterborough on 7 July 1962.

Britannia No. 70038 *Robin Hood* is captured near Hornsey with the 7.43 Cleethorpes to King's Cross on 7 July 1962.

Prototype Type 4 D0280 *Falcon* is spotted at Finsbury Park on the 15.15 King's Cross to Sheffield on 7 July 1962.

A unique service on the Brighton main line was the weekday steam-hauled 17.25 London Bridge to Reading and Tonbridge via Redhill in among the electric business services. There was an operational problem in getting the returning locomotive off of the conditional 12.50 stone trains from Woking to New Cross Gate back to Redhill, with it having to be scheduled after rush hour. However, to avoid the rostering of an additional set of men it became the unofficial practice to attach this loco as a pilot to the 17.25 at London Bridge, resulting in some smart working at Redhill in not only splitting the train, but also detaching the pilot. On the 12th, N Class No. 31862 was used to pilot U Class No. 31807 and was seen at Coulsdon North. On the 14th a brief visit to Doncaster was made. Working freights were O1 Class No. 63646 and O2/4 No. 63935. A visit to Leighton Buzzard took place on the 28th, where two Duchesses were seen working: No. 46221 *Queen Elizabeth* on the 13.30 Euston to Perth and No. 46225 *Duchess of Gloucester* with a Down relief to Liverpool. Duchess No. 46228 *Duchess of Rutland* had recently arrived at Euston, while at Leighton Buzzard Class 5 No. 44685 was working the 9.05 Llandudno to Euston, and sister No. 45230 was on the 10.45 Hastings to Walsall via Clapham Junction. On the 29th I had permits to visit Camden Town, Willesden and Kentish Town sheds. In the long shed at Camden was the soon-to-be-withdrawn Princess Royal Class No. 46209 *Princess Beatrice*, as well as Duchesses Nos 46240 *City of Coventry* and 46245 *City of London*. Also present was the relatively short-lived Type 4 prototype DP2. Royal Scot No. 46135 *The East Lancashire Regiment* was also seen. Several stored withdrawn locomotives were present at Willesden, including

N Class No. 31862 and U Class No. 31807 are spotted at Coulsdon North on the 17.25 London Bridge to Reading and Tonbridge on 12 July 1962. The track veering off to the left went to the now closed Coulsdon North station, the terminus of the LBSCR overhead electric lines. The double track to the left is the Redhill avoiding line via Quarry Tunnel, and the sidings to the right went to Hall & Co.'s Coulsdon Quarry.

O1 No. 63646 is seen at Doncaster on 14 July 1962.

Also spotted at Doncaster on 14 July 1962 is O2/4 No. 3935.

Left: Duchess No. 46221 *Queen Elizabeth* is photographed near Leighton Buzzard with the 13.30 Euston to Perth on 28 July 1962.

Below: Duchess No. 46240 *City Of Coventry* stands in Camden Town shed on 29 July 1962.

Prototype Type 4 DP2 is seen at Camden Town on 29 July 1962.

Fowler Class 3 tanks Nos 40049 and 40080, Stanier Class 3 tanks Nos 40144 and 40157, Stanier Class 4 tanks Nos 42470 and 42576, and LNWR G2 No. 49413. Also present were Caprotti Class 5 No. 44752, Royal Scot No. 46163 *Civil Service Rifleman* and Jubilee No. 45592 *Indore,* as well as a recently repainted 'Jinty', No. 47307. The weather had turned quite gloomy by the time I got to Kentish Town, where three Standard Class 2 tanks – Nos 84005, 84008 and 84029 – were in open storage and Caprotti Standard 5 No. 73140 from Rowsley was being coaled.

    I travelled to Templecombe on 4 August with the intention of seeing the Somerset & Dorset 7F 2-8-0s and the LMS 4Fs that had been built for them. I was in luck as Class 7F No. 53810 was on the 10.42 Exmouth to Cleethorpes, while 4F No. 44558 worked the 12.23 to Bournemouth West and 4F No. 44559 double-headed Standard 4 4-6-0 No. 75009 on the 7.00 Cleethorpes to Exmouth. On 10 August I made a short trip to Finsbury Park. On the way there I stopped off at Clapham Junction in time to see Merchant Navy No. 35012 *United States Lines* go past on the Down Atlantic Coast Express. I only recorded three sightings at Finsbury Park – A3 No. 60044 *Melton* on the 12.25 King's Cross to Newcastle, A3 No. 60065 *Knight of Thistle* on the 12.45 King's Cross to Leeds and Britannia No. 70038 *Robin Hood* on the 8.32 from Cleethorpes. A short visit was made to Kettering on the 11th, where LMS Class 5s were very much in evidence, with No. 44861 working the 12.08 Nottingham to St Pancras, No. 45134 working the 12.55 St Pancras to Nottingham and No. 45333 working the 14.00 Kettering to Leicester. On the 18th I had a permit to visit Old Oak Common sheds, and

Fowler Class 3 tank No. 40049 is seen stored at Willesden on 29 July 1962 after its withdrawal.

Stanier Class 4 tank No. 42576 is also seen stored at Willesden on 29 July 1962 after its withdrawal.

LNWR G2 No. 49413 withdrawn at Willesden on 29 July 1962.

Jubilee Class No. 45592 *Indore* at Willesden on 29 July 1962.

Left: 'Jinty'
No. 47307 is seen
at Willesden on
29 July 1962.

Below: Standard 2
tank No. 84005
stored at Kentish
Town on
29 July 1962.

Caprotti Standard 5 No. 73140 is at Kentish Town on 29 July 1962.

Class 7F No. 53810 leaves Templecombe with the 10.42 Exmouth to Cleethorpes on 4 August 1962.

Merchant Navy No. 35012 *United States Lines* leaves Clapham Junction with the Down Atlantic Coast Express on 10 August 1962.

A3 No. 60065 *Knight of Thistle* is seen near Finsbury Park on the 12.45 King's Cross to Leeds on 10 August 1962.

LMS Class 5 No. 45134 is captured near Kettering with the 12.55 St Pancras to Nottingham on 11 August 1962.

this was a hot, sunny day. Again several withdrawn stored locos were present, including Castles Nos 5082 *Swordfish* and 5084 *Reading Abbey*, Class 5700 Nos 8761, 8763 and 8773, and condensing Class 5700 No. 9709. Several other Castles were seen, including Nos 4082 *Windsor Castle,* 4088 *Dartmouth Castle,* 5018 *St Mawes Castle* and 7037 *Swindon.* Additionally, three Standard 4 tanks – No. 80105, No. 80134 and No. 80135 (ex-Tilbury) – were stored awaiting works and reallocation, while the first Western diesel-hydraulic, D1000 *Western Enterprise* in experimental 'Desert Sand' livery, was also seen.

Back to Hitchin again on the 25th, the A3s were having a field day with No. 60044 *Melton* on the 14.10 King's Cross to Bradford, No. 60073 *St Gatien* on the 9.04 Sunderland to King's Cross, No. 60103 *Flying Scotsman* with the 13.50 King's Cross to Newcastle, No. 60105 *Victor Wild* on the 1340 King's Cross to Leeds and No. 60106 *Flying Fox* on the 10.05 Bradford to King's Cross. B1 No. 61073 headed the 14.15 King's Cross to Skegness while another B1, No. 61179, was on the 12.05 Skegness to King's Cross. Britannia No. 70038 *Robin Hood* was in charge of the 9.43 from Cleethorpes – a regular duty for this loco – while V2 No. 60814 was on the 10.50 Leeds to King's Cross. Indeed, this was a fine day for steam!

Saturday 1 September was the last Saturday of the 1962 summer service and I was at Basingstoke to see many of the extra services and unusual workings for that day. Of special interest were Urie S15 No. 30512 on the 10.45 Waterloo to the West of England, Urie S15 No. 30497 on the 11.54 Waterloo to the West of England, King Arthur No. 30782 *Sir Brian* with the 9.40 Ilfracombe to Waterloo and Lord Nelson

Castle Class 4082 *Windsor Castle* in Old Oak Common shed on 19 August 1962.

5700 Class Nos 8763 and 8773 stand in Old Oak Common shed on 19 August 1962.

Still with GWR on the tank sides, condensing Class 5700 No. 9709 is seen at Old Oak Common shed on 19 August 1962.

Standard 4 tank No. 80135 is seen stored at Old Oak Common on 19 August 1962.

Castle 5084 *Reading Abbey* is spotted at Old Oak Common on 18 August 1962.

A3 No. 60073 *St Gatien* is spotted south of Hitchin on the 9.04 Sunderland to King's Cross
on 25 August 1962.

B1 No. 61073 is seen near Hitchin with the 14.15 King's Cross to Skegness on 25 August 1962.

Britannia No. 70038 *Robin Hood* is captured near Hitchin on the 9.43 Cleethorpes to King's Cross on 25 August 1962.

V2 No. 60814 is spotted south of Hitchin with the 10.50 Leeds to King's Cross on 25 August 1962.

Urie S15 No. 30512 is spotted near Worting Junction with the 10.45 Waterloo to the West of England on 1 September 1962.

No. 30861 *Lord Anson* on the 11.51 Southampton Dock to Waterloo. However, the finest sight was of Schools No. 30925 *Cheltenham* on the 10.15 Waterloo to the West of England. The 10.15 Down had been a regular Schools turn. *Cheltenham* worked as far as Exeter Central, with this ten-coach train arriving three minutes early. The return was made the following day on the 8.25 Plymouth to Waterloo. Although I did not see it on the 2nd, *Lord Anson* worked the Southern Counties Society's 'South Western Limited' from Waterloo to Sidmouth Junction and then from Exeter Central to Salisbury. A short visit was made to Reading General on the 8th, where three Castles were seen: No. 5017 *The Gloucestershire Regiment 28th, 61st* with the 12.35 Weston-super-Mare to Paddington, No. 5018 *St Mawes Castle* on the 12.05 Hereford to Paddington and No. 5055 *Earl of Eldon* on the 11.15 Minehead to Paddington. Additionally, King Class No. 6019 *King Henry V* headed the 7.30 Penzance to Paddington. On the 15th I went to Holmethorpe, between Redhill and Merstham, to photograph U1 No. 31901 joining the main line with the 10.38 freight from Merstham to Horley. In fact, I was actually on my way to Potters Bar, where A4s No. 60013 *Dominion of New Zealand* and No. 60033 *Seagull* were working the 9.30 Newcastle to King's Cross and a Down relief respectively. Here, the 13.20 Peterborough to King's Cross was hauled by V2 No. 60906 and the 14.45 freight Ferme Park to Werrington by Standard 9 No. 92146.

Castle No. 5017 *The Gloucestershire Regiment 28th, 61st* at Reading General with the 12.35 Weston-super-Mare to Paddington on 8 September 1962.

Castle No. 5055 *Earl of Eldon* entering Reading General with the 11.15 Minehead to Paddington on 8 September 1962.

U1 No. 31901 passes Holmethorpe signal box with the 10.38 Merstham to Horley freight on 15 September 1962.

A4 No. 60013 *Dominion of New Zealand* is seen near Potters Bar on the 9.30 Newcastle to King's Cross on 15 September 1962.

A4 No. 60033 *Seagull* is also near Potters Bar on a Down relief on 15 September 1962.

Near Potters Bar, Class 9 No. 92146 passes by with the 14.45 freight Ferme Park to Werrington on 15 September 1962.

It was interesting to note the sight of Derby Type 4 diesel D171 on the 15.20 King's Cross to Leeds, having earlier seen it working the Up Yorkshire Pullman, proving the effectiveness of using diesel or electric locomotives on main line services. More shed permits were obtained for the 22nd, this time to Norwood Junction, Nine Elms and Stewarts Lane. I was hoping to meet one of my uncles at Norwood but he was not rostered to work that day. In open storage were U1 No. 31904 and Ws Nos 31921 and 31925. The two Ws were to remain in service until the end of 1963, whereas No. 31904 was withdrawn, together with the majority of the class, at the end of 1962. At Stewarts Lane the allocation was very much reduced and the only locos noted were N Class No. 31827, Standard 5 No. 73072 and Standard 4 tank No. 80034; Nine Elms was much busier, with E4 Class No. 32473, which had been spruced up shortly before its purchase by the Bluebell Railway, the stock workings from Clapham Junction to and from Waterloo had become the responsibility of ex-GWR 5700 Class Pannier tanks, two being Nos 4698 and 9770, and M7s, including No. 30378, which were later to be withdrawn in December. Also present were Q1s Nos 33008 and 33040, Standard 5 No. 73042 and a crop of Bulleid Pacifics.

Wood Green on 6 October was an overcast affair. A3 No. 60108 *Gay Crusader* was on the 7.40 Bradford to Kings's Cross and Britannia No. 70040 *Clive of India* was working the 8.32 ex-Cleethorpes. The 11.35 Ferme Park to New England was worked by V2 No. 60808 while two Class 9s, Nos 92184 and 92185 headed an Up freight and the 12.15 Ferme Park to New England respectively. Then it was to White Hart Lane

W Class No. 31921 is seen stored at Norwood Junction shed on 22 September 1962.

Standard 5 No. 73042 is seen at Stewarts Lane shed on 22 September 1962.

5700 Class No. 4659 stands at Nine Elms shed on 22 September 1962.

Q1 No. 33040 is also at Nine Elms shed on 22 September 1962.

to watch Tottenham Hotspur draw 4-4 with Arsenal! On the 7th 'The Sussex Special Rail Tour' was run by the RCTS, Schools Class No. 30925 *Cheltenham* had a one-hour schedule from London Bridge to Brighton, E6 No. 32418 and A1x No. 32636 worked to Seaford and back (the E6 doing most of the work) and finally a return to London Bridge via Steyning and Dorking was made behind K Class No. 32353. Also on the 7th, K Class No. 32344, possibly ex-Eastleigh works, double-headed Q1 No. 33024 on the 12.10 special freight from Eastleigh to Newhaven, being seen at Barnham. Sadly, both K Class locos were to be withdrawn by the end of 1962. On the 10th The 'Victory Belle' ran from Victoria to Sheffield Park via Haywards Heath and Ardingly; the restored T9 Class 120 was the train engine to and from Haywards Heath, while A1x 55 *Stepney* and Adams tank No. 488 worked from Haywards Heath to Sheffield Park and return. More withdrawn, or soon to be withdrawn locos were present at Eastleigh on the 27th. These included USA Class No. 30065 (later to enter service stock as DS237 *Maunsell*), Urie S15 No. 30505, all three Beattie Tanks (Nos 30585, 30586 and 30587), the last King Arthur, No. 30770 *Sir Prianius*, and O2 No. 30199; possibly fresh from the paint shop were M7s Nos 30052, 30029 and 30480, U Class No. 31613 and modified West Country No. 34038 *Lynton*. Three W Class tanks were on shed including No. 31912, which was waiting to go to Exmouth Junction as one of the replacements for the Z Class 0-8-0 tanks, as well as Class 9 No. 92231. The Class 9s were used on the heavy freights from the Fawley Oil Plant.

V2 No. 60808 is captured near Wood Green on the 11.35 Ferme Park to New England freight on 6 October 1962.

Right: Class 9 No. 92185 is seen near Wood Green with the 12.15 Ferme Park to New England freight on 6 October 1962.

Below: Schools Class No. 30925 *Cheltenham* approaches Patcham Tunnel with the RCTS 'Sussex Special Rail Tour' on 7 October 1962.

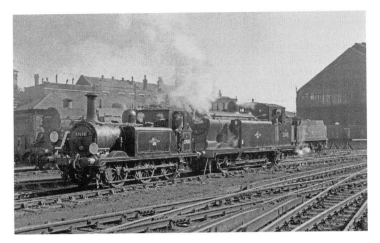

E6 No. 32428 and A1x
No. 32636 are seen
preparing to work the
RCTS 'Sussex Special Rail
Tour' at Brighton shed
on 7 October 1962.

K No. 32344 is seen
double-heading Q1
No. 33024 near Barnham
on the 12.10 Eastleigh to
Newhaven special freight
on 7 October 1962.

A1x No. 55 *Stepney* and
Adams tank No. 488
are captured near
Copyhold Junction with
the 'Victory Belle' on
21 October 1962.

USA No. 30065 stands at Eastleigh on 27 October 1962.

Beattie tanks Nos 30585 and 30587 are also seen at Eastleigh on 27 October 1962.

B4 Class No. 30102 is spotted at Eastleigh on 27 October 1962.

Also seen at Eastleigh on 27 October 1962 is Urie S15 No. 30505.

Class 9 No. 92231 is captured at Eastleigh, also on 27 October 1962.

Ex-works M7 No. 30052 stands at Eastleigh on 27 October 1962.

Come a slightly misty 3 November I was at Wivelsfield to catch K Class No. 32347 on the 13.49 engineers' train from Three Bridges to Barnham. This was the last time I was to see one of this class of locomotive in action since it was one of nine to be withdrawn in December 1962.

My last visit of 1962 was to Eastleigh on 8 December, which was not a very good day in many respects. Firstly the weather was poor, secondly I had recently bought a 35-mm single-lens reflex camera that was not performing as I had hoped and, more importantly, responsibility for British Railways was to be transferred from the British Transport Commission to the British Railways Board on the 31st. The accountants were in full flow and had decreed the Southern Region had too many steam locomotives, meaning that just under 100 had to be withdrawn, irrespective of their mechanical condition and when they had last been in works. As a result the last King Arthur was to go (though it was probably due anyway), as were all eight Class Z locos (again, they were due to be withdrawn since most needed new fireboxes and W Class locos, redundant in the London area, were being sent to replace them). The remaining G16 tanks and the two H16 tanks, which were again redundant, also had to go, and the three Beattie tanks had been replaced by GWR 1366 Class locomotives. There was nothing really surprising in those withdrawals, but what was unexpected was the withdrawal of the remaining 700 Class engines, including those designated for snowplough duties, as well as the remaining Schools Class locos and all of the K Class locomotives. At the time of the announcement of these withdrawals I worked in an office adjacent to that of the Motive Power section at Essex House, and they were unaware that the withdrawal of the Ks

K Class No. 32347 at Wivelsfield with the 13.49 Three Bridges to Barnham engineers' train on 3 November 1962.

was due, especially since a number had been through works in 1961 and 1962. In some respects this was the start of the storage of withdrawn locomotives that could not be broken up in railway workshops – certainly as far as the Southern Region was concerned. From December 1962 until mid-1963 at least fifteen locos were stored in Hove Goods yard before being towed away – the shape of things to come. When I visited Eastleigh on that bleak day the following were waiting their fate: K Class No. 32352, Schools No. 30937, Urie S15 No. 30502, Z No. 30953, G16 No. 30495, King Arthur No. 30770, K Nos 32344, 32346 and 32350, Schools No. 30929, M7 No. 30045, G16 No. 30494, USA No. 30070 (later to become service stock DS238 *Wainwright)*, M7 No. 30131, 700 Class No. 30316, USA DS234 (withdrawn as No. 30062 in November and reinstated into service stock) and many, many more. Ex-works Merchant Navy No. 35011 *General Steam Navigation* brightened the scene somewhat, while a visitor from Nottingham was Class 9 No. 92112. This was a sad end to the year for this 'Brighton man'. As Bob Dylan said, 'The times they are a-changing.'

Again at Eastleigh, K Class No. 32352 is seen on 8 December 1962.

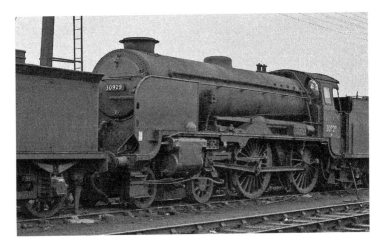

Schools No. 30929
Malvern stands at
Eastleigh on 8
December 1962.

King Arthur No. 30770
Sir Prianius is
photographed at Eastleigh
8 December 1962.

Looking a little worn,
K Class No. 32350 is also
at Eastleigh 8
December 1962.

M7 No. 30045 is spotted at Eastleigh on 8 December 1962.

Z Class No. 30953 is seen at Eastleigh on 8 December 1962.

USA Class DS234 is also seen at Eastleigh on 8 December 1962.

Sources and Dedication

Except where indicated, all photographs were taken by myself and in the main have not been previously published. An unknown box camera was used for all prior to August 1955; between August 1955 and 1958 a Purma Plus camera was used with mainly Kodak Super XX, Ilford FP3 or Agfa Isopan ISS film; a Zeiss Werra 35-mm rangefinder was used between 19 and 22 April 1962 with Kodak Plus X film; the photographs from Eastleigh on 8 December 1962 were taken using a Reflexa SLR with HP3 film; and for the remainder the camera was a Montaus Ultraflex TLR, with films including Kodak Verichrome, Tri-X, and Ilford FP3 and HP3.

Reference in passing has been made to the following publications:

Longworth, Hugh, *British Railways Steam Locomotives 1948–1969* (OPC, 2010).
Bradley, D. L., *Locomotives of the LSWR, SER, SECR, LBSCR, LCDR and Southern Railway* (RCTS various dates).
Various Ian Allan *ABCs*.
Verrall, Charlie, *Steam around Basingstoke and Salisbury* (Amberley Publishing, 2017).

Reference has been made to the files at www.sixbellsjunction.co.uk for details of the various railtours seen. In addition, visits have been made to www.brdatabase.com for confirmation of individual locomotive allocations.

Thanks have to go to all the railway workers who never queried as to why I was wandering along the track or round the depots. Thanks also to my co-workers at Redhill and Essex House, especially the fellow photographers who encouraged me to restart photographing railways in 1961. Sadly, most of them are no longer on this mortal coil.

Many thanks go to Brian Read, who took on the sterling task of checking the original draft text, and to Mick Hymans for help in providing information from his collection of magazines, etc., often at short notice.

This book is dedicated to the late Pat Farmer, who was with me on the Lickley Limited in 1955, and to the late Chris Gammell; without his suggestion I would not have digitalised my images and this book would not have been produced. Finally, to David Hey, who died while this book was being prepared. David kindly invited me to contribute to his website http://www.davidheyscollection.com/index.htm – a project we sadly cannot now complete.

Thanks also have to go to the good people at Amberley Publishing for their encouragement and responses to my queries.

Special thanks to my wife Gillian for bearing with me while I spent so much time hidden away on the computer, and to my youngest son, Jeremy, who checked the printer's proofs for me.

Finally, thanks to you, the reader, for getting this far.

To be continued…